Classic Asian Fashion Coloring Book

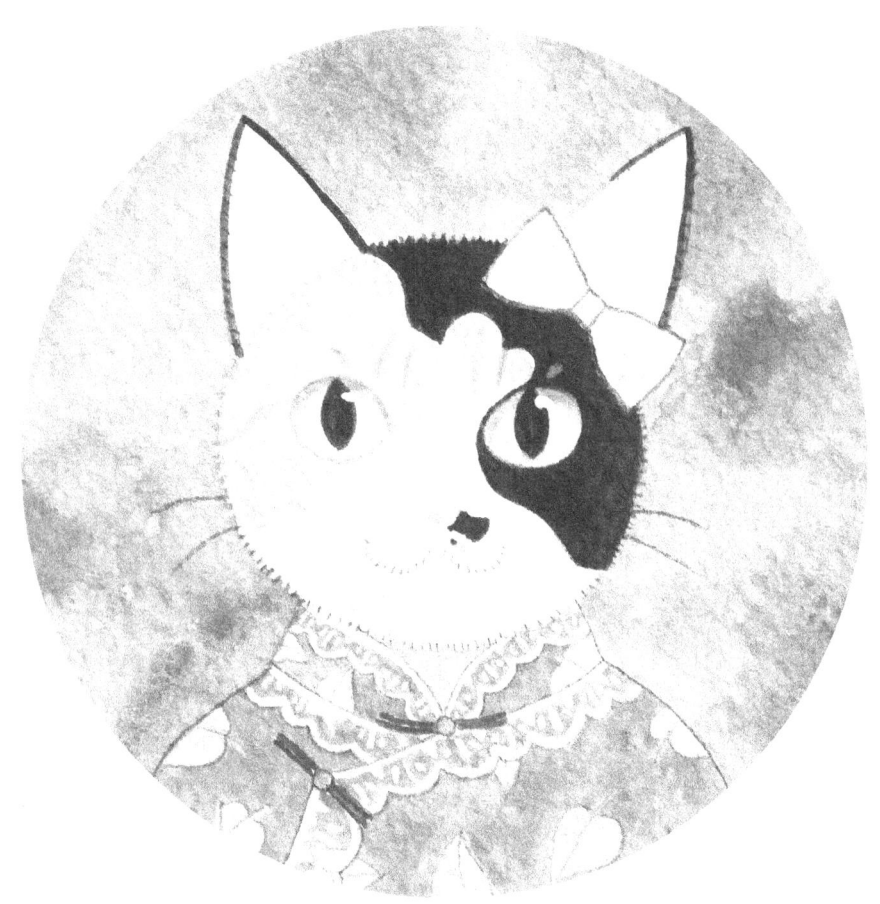

Illustrator: Vivian Liao
Author / Design: Lance Derrick
Publishing: Colokara

Copyright © 2018 Colokara

All rights reserved. No part of this book may be reproduced in any form on by an electronic or mechanical means, including information storage and retrieval systems, without permission in writing from the publisher, except by a reviewer who may quote brief passages in a review.

Steps to a Relaxing Coloring

As an adult, you can enjoy coloring just as much as you did as a child. To make it a truly relaxing experience, try following these steps:

1. Find a quiet space. It's easier to focus on what you are doing when there are no distraction.
2. Organize your materials. Lay out your coloring book and crayons or pens.
3. Set the mood. Turn on some tranquil music, diffuse lavender or another relaxing oil and make sure you have your preferred drink at hand.
4. Select your picture. Which image speaks to you today? That's the one you should color.
5. Choose your palette. Select the colors you will be using for your image.
6. Begin coloring. This is the fun part. Don't worry about getting everything perfect, just start.

Allow yourself to relax and focus on the coloring. You'll find it is an amazing way to alleviate stress and take a little time out from the day's hassles. If you feel don't want to do it anymore, just stop!

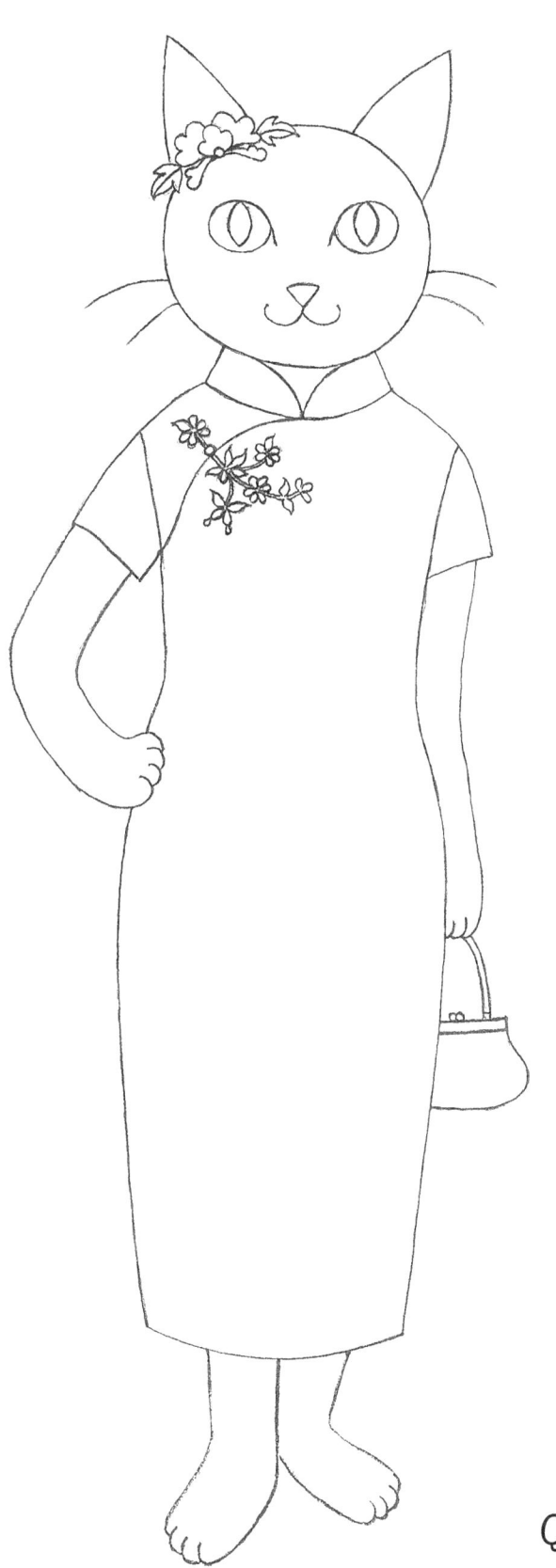

Qipao, China

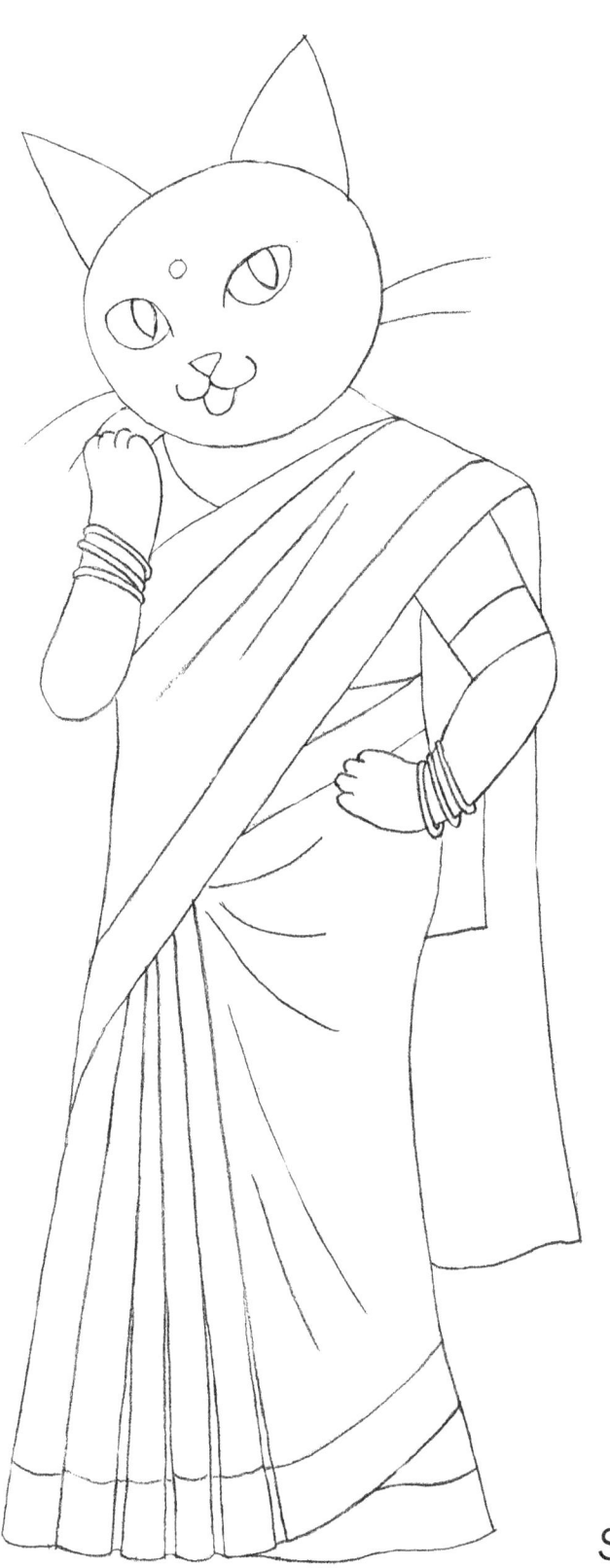

Sari, India

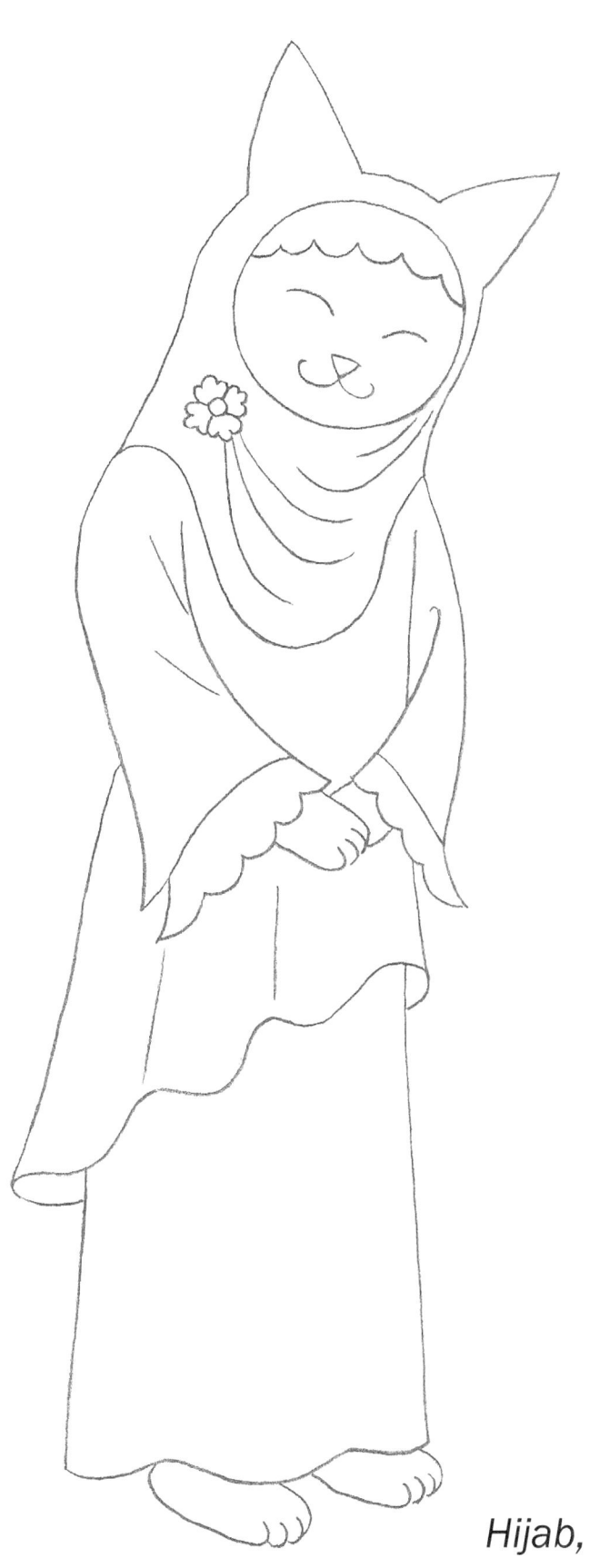

Hijab, Indonesia

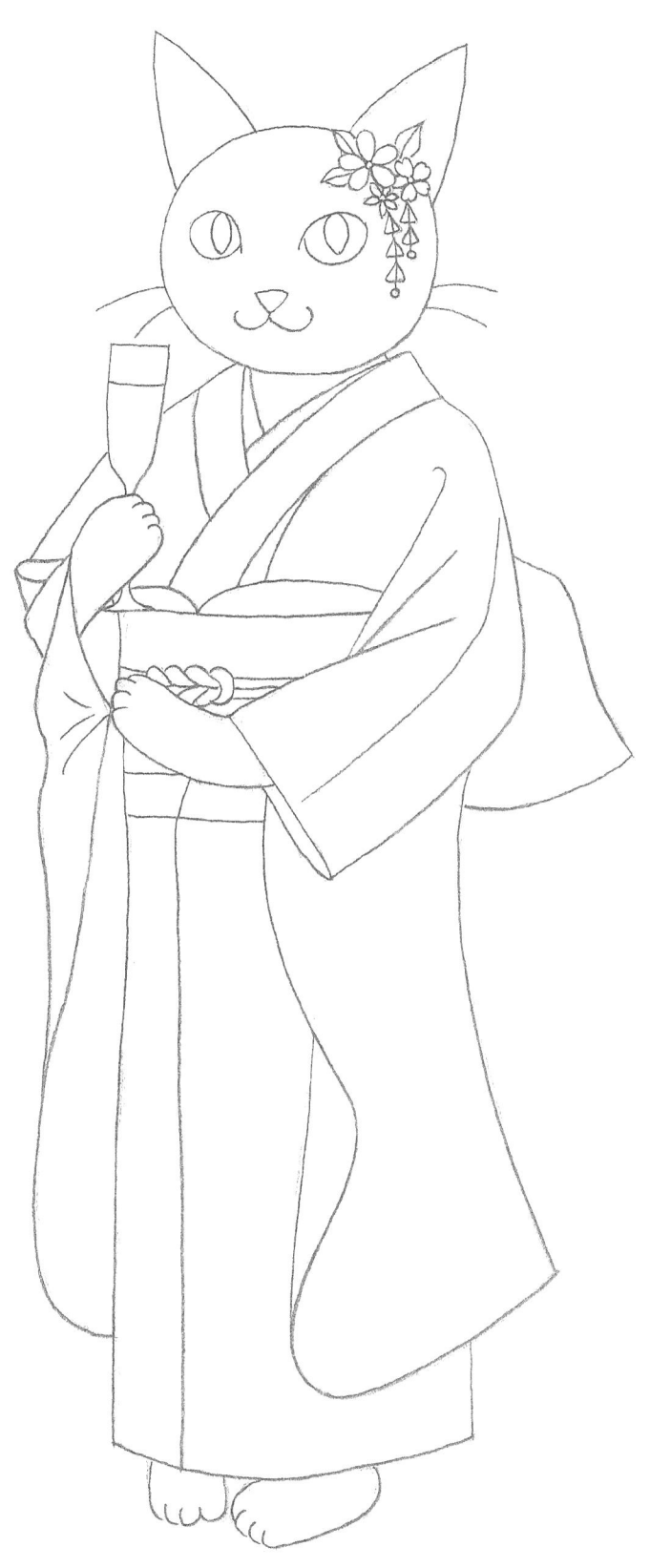

Furisode Kimono. Japan

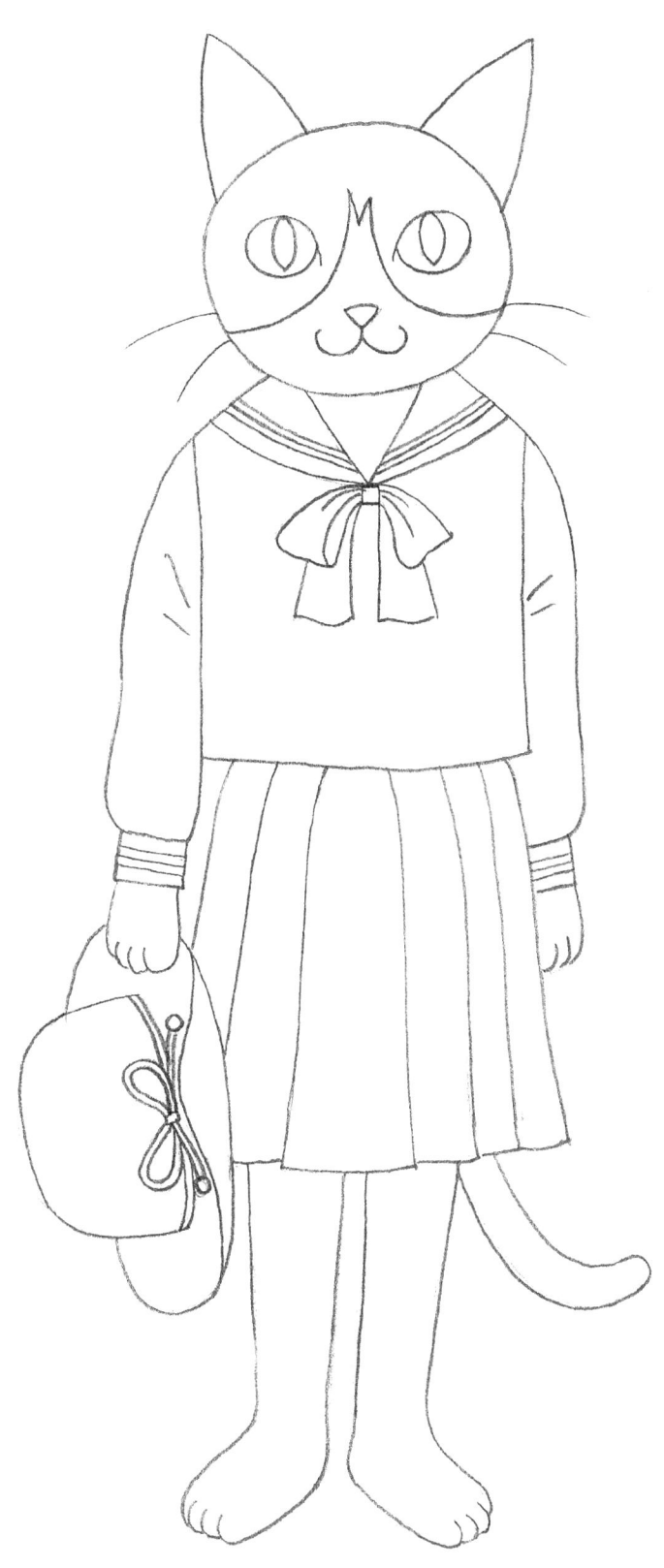

Uniform. Japan

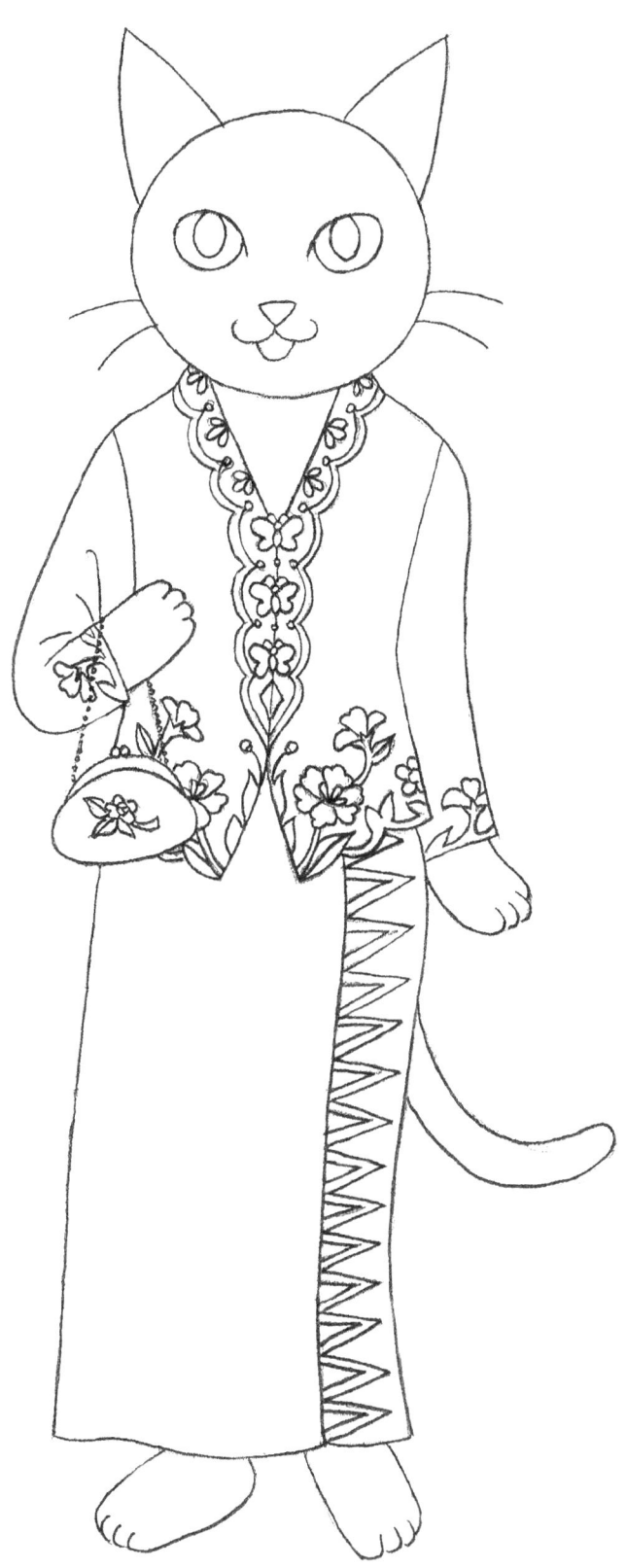

Nyonya Kebaya, Malaysia

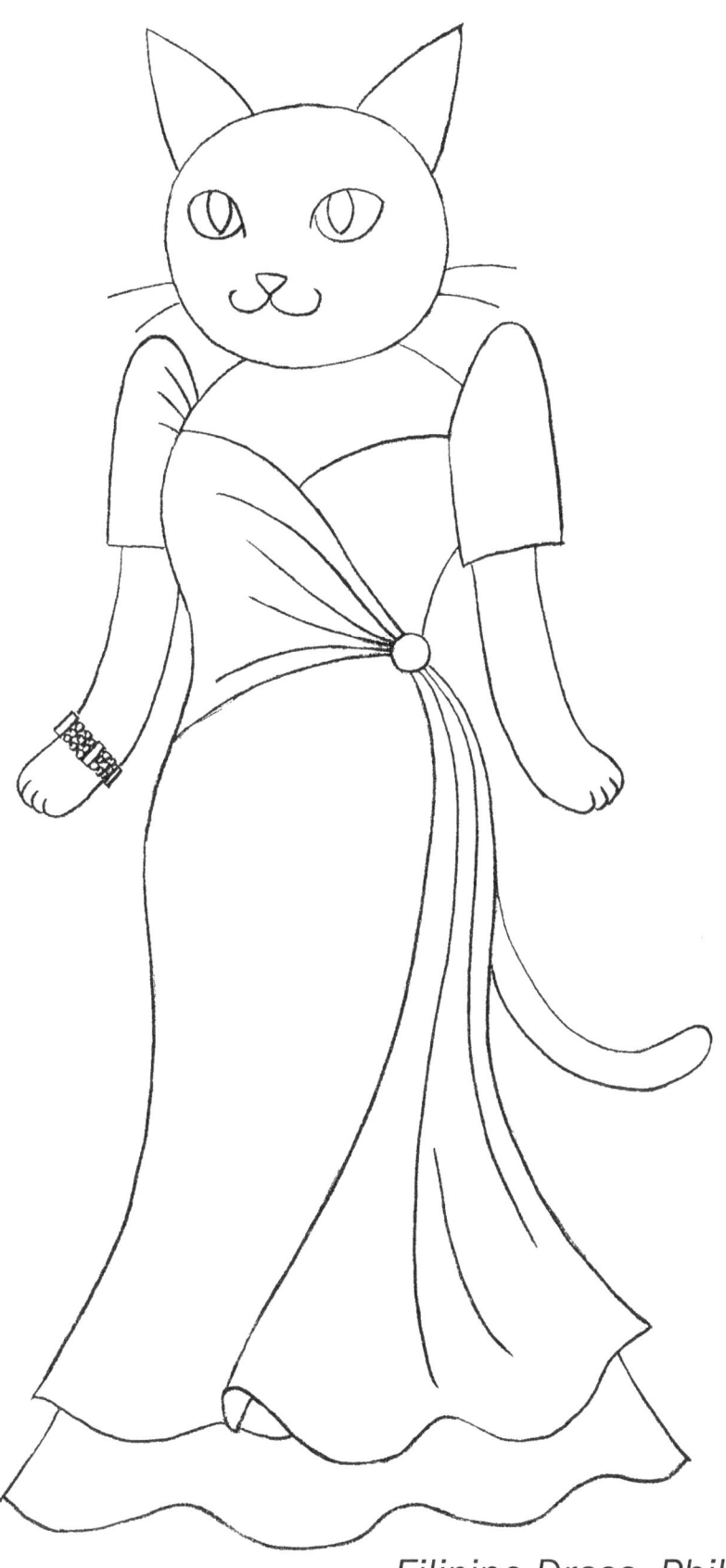

Filipino Dress, Philippines

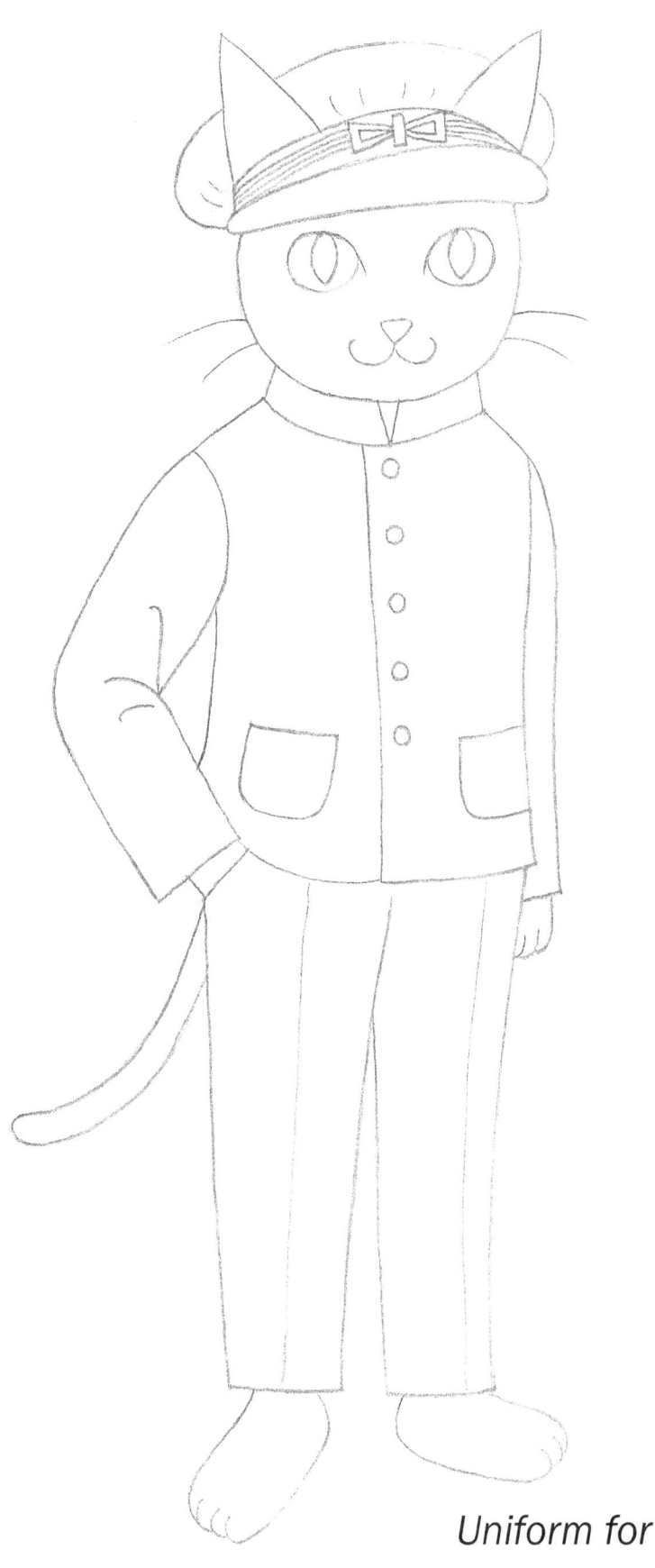

Uniform for Boy, Taiwan

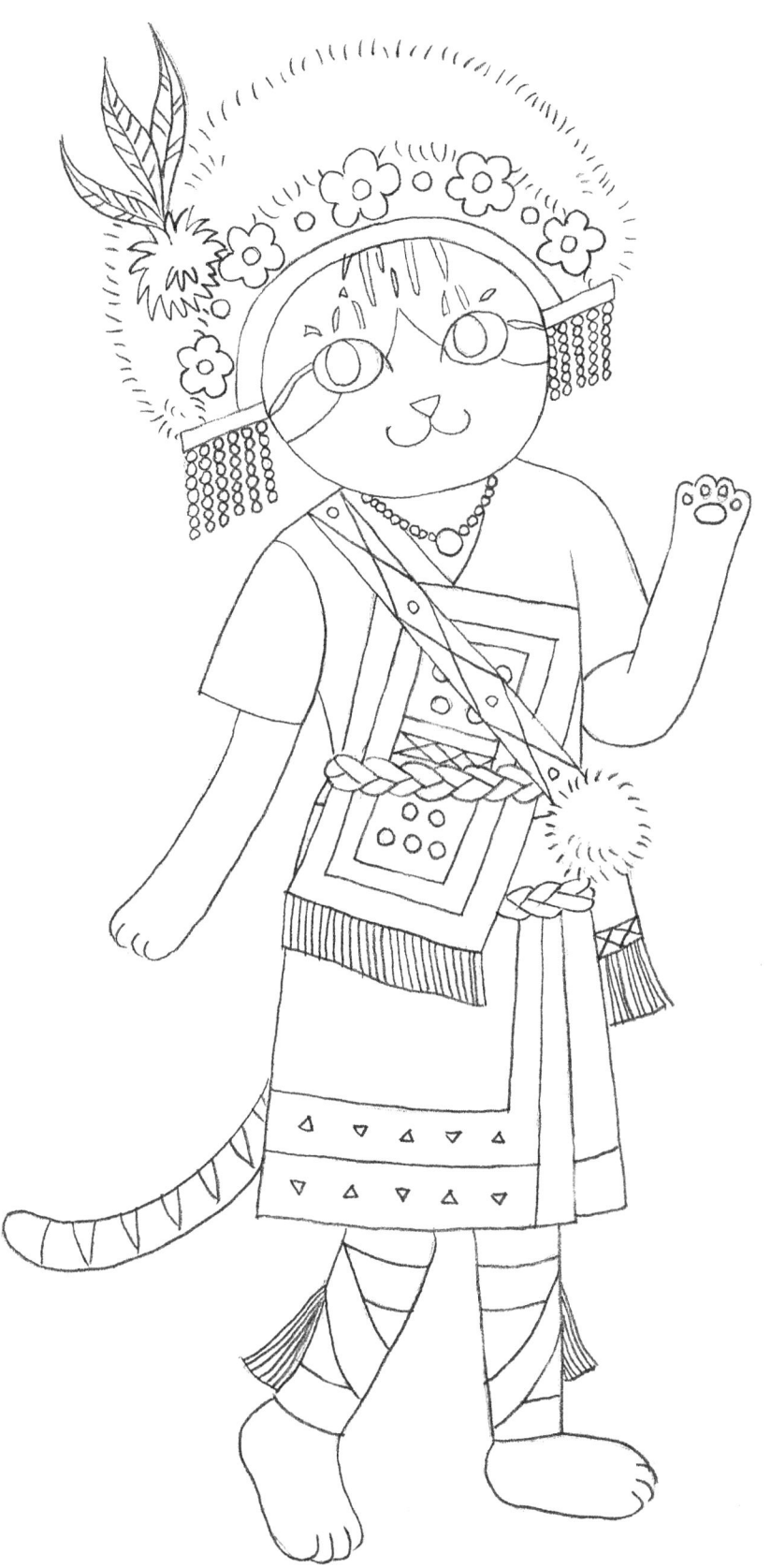

Amis, Taiwan

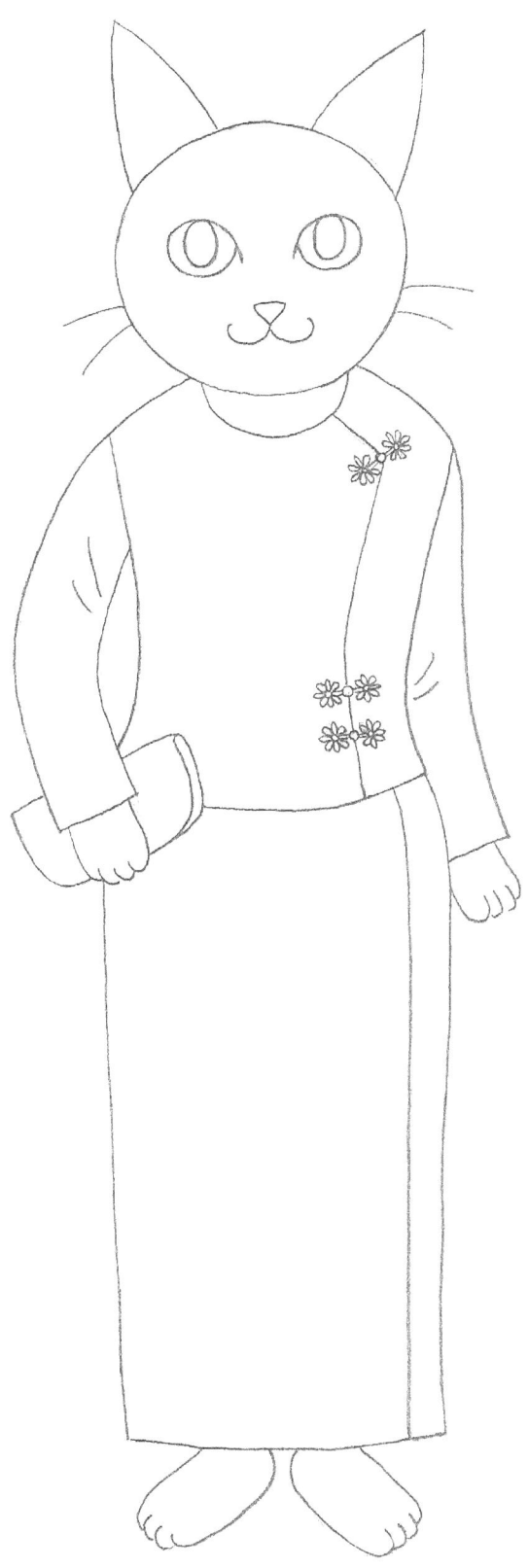

Myanmar, Taiwan

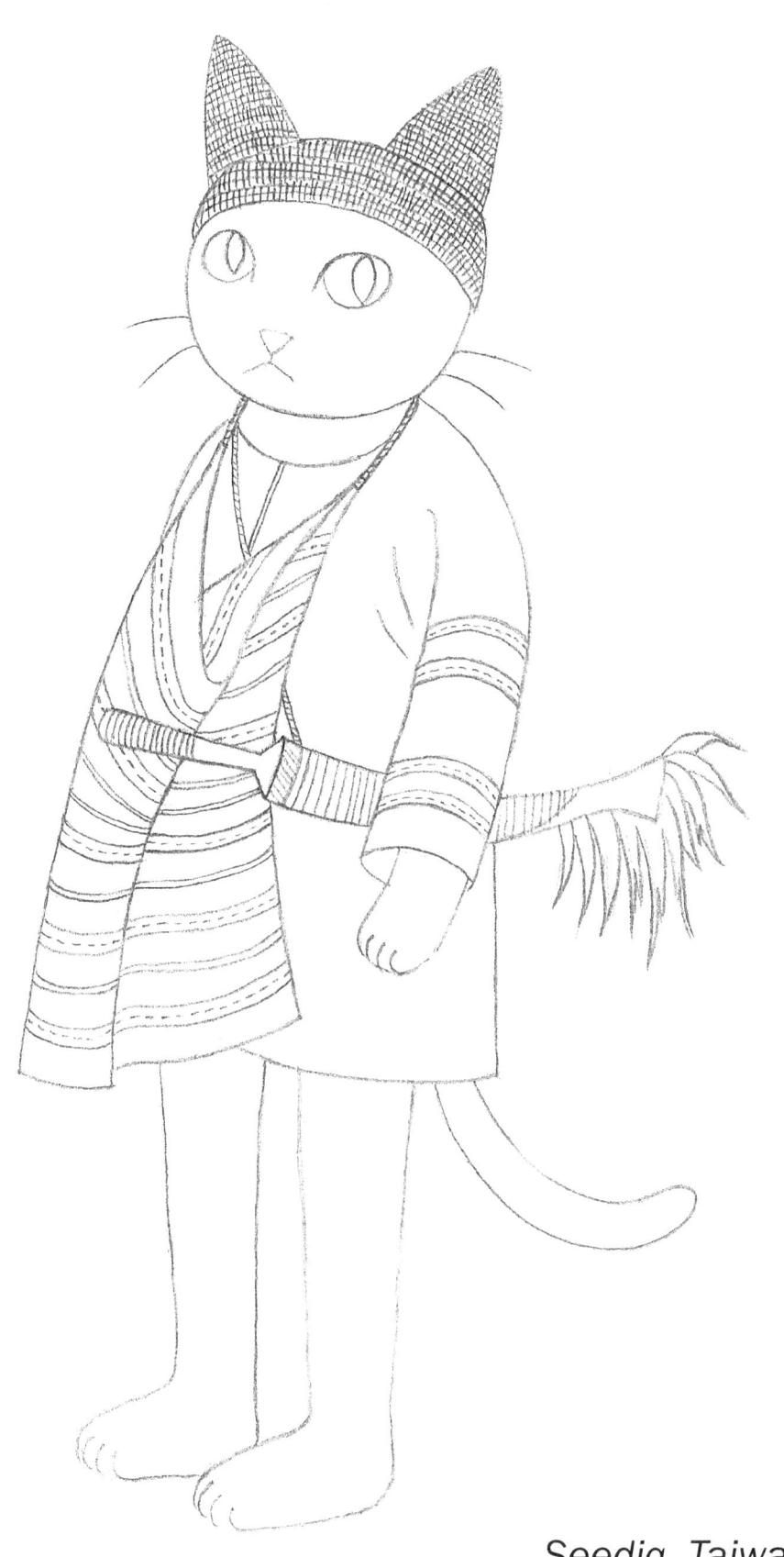

Seediq, Taiwan

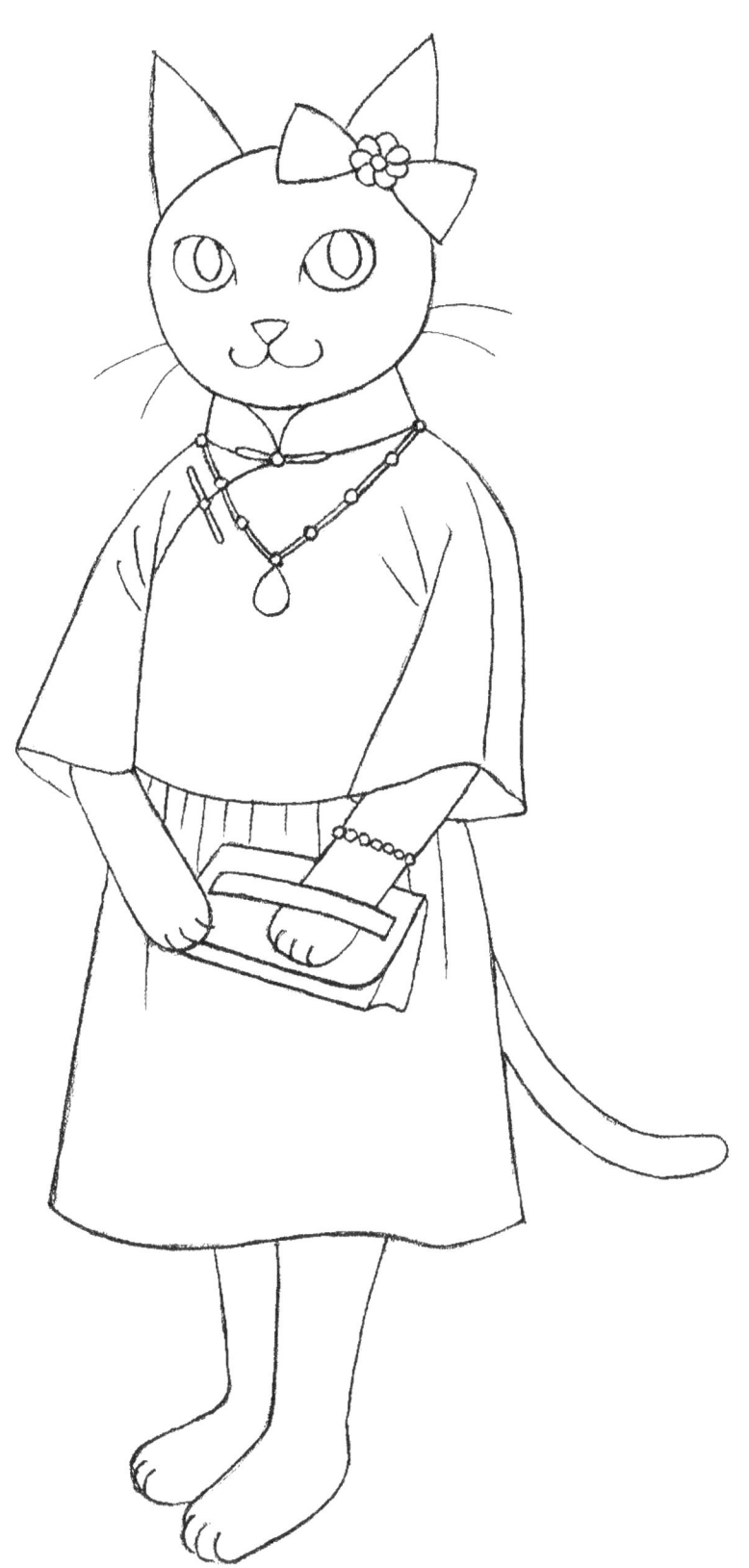

Taiwanese

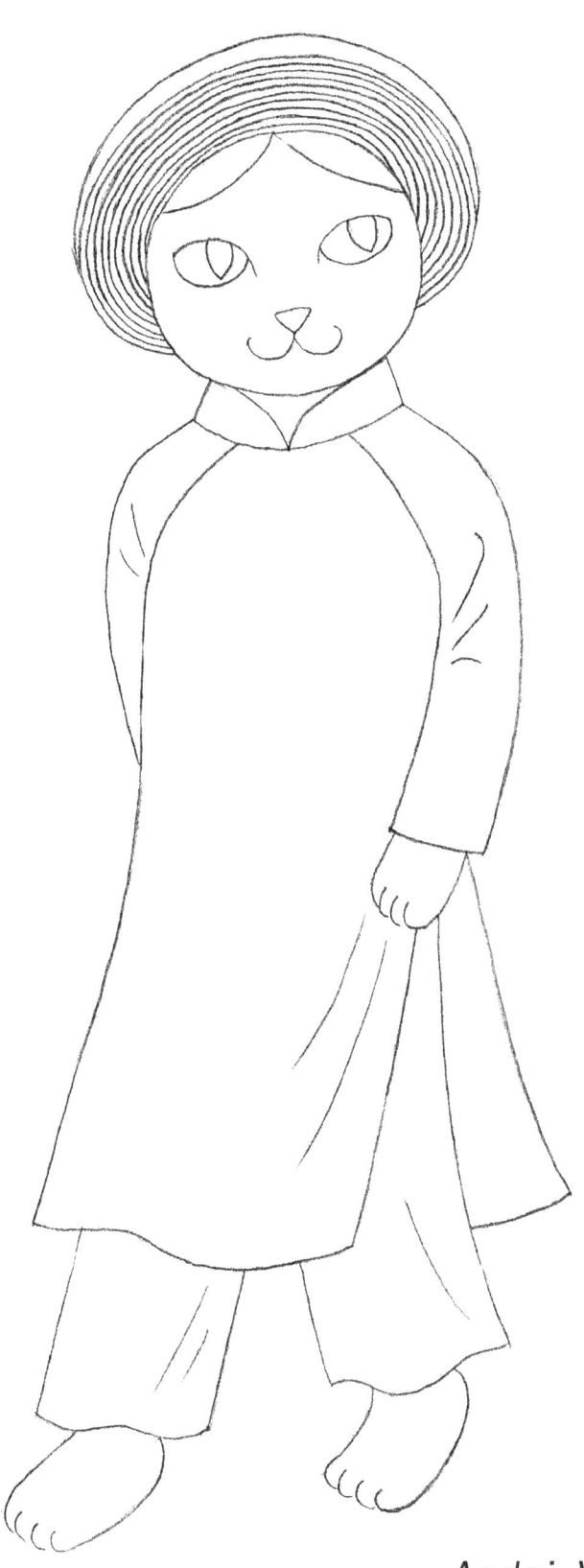

Aodai, Vietnam

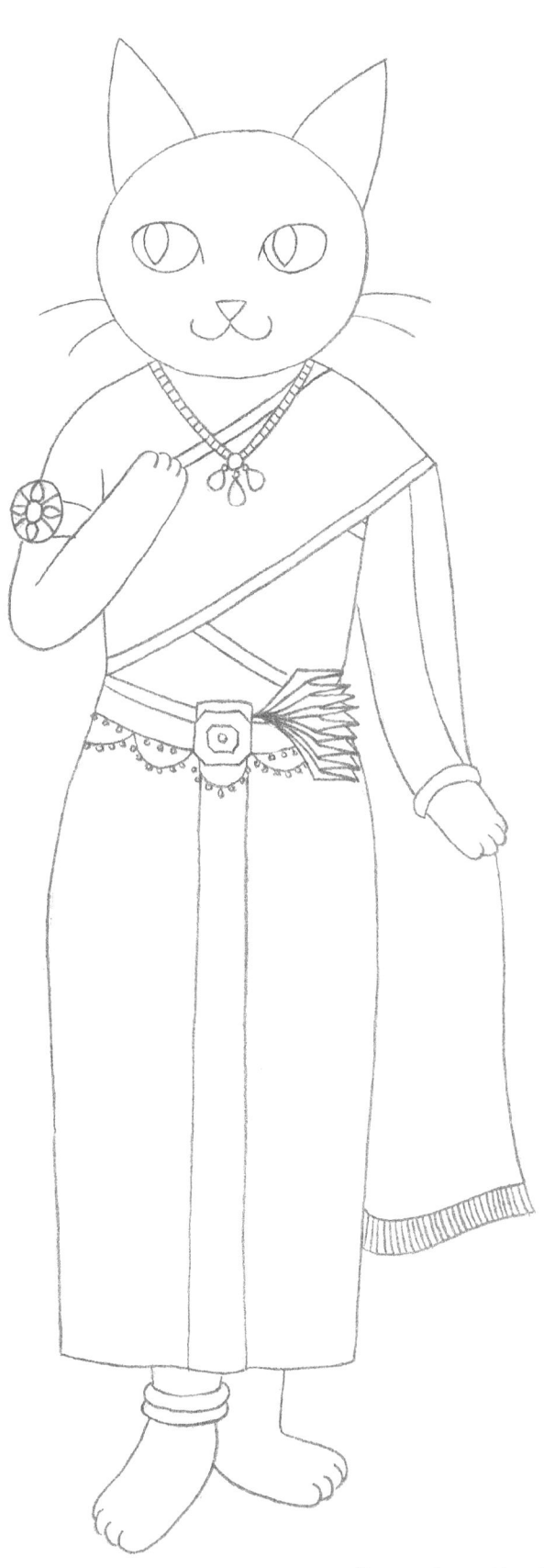

Cambodia Wedding Dress

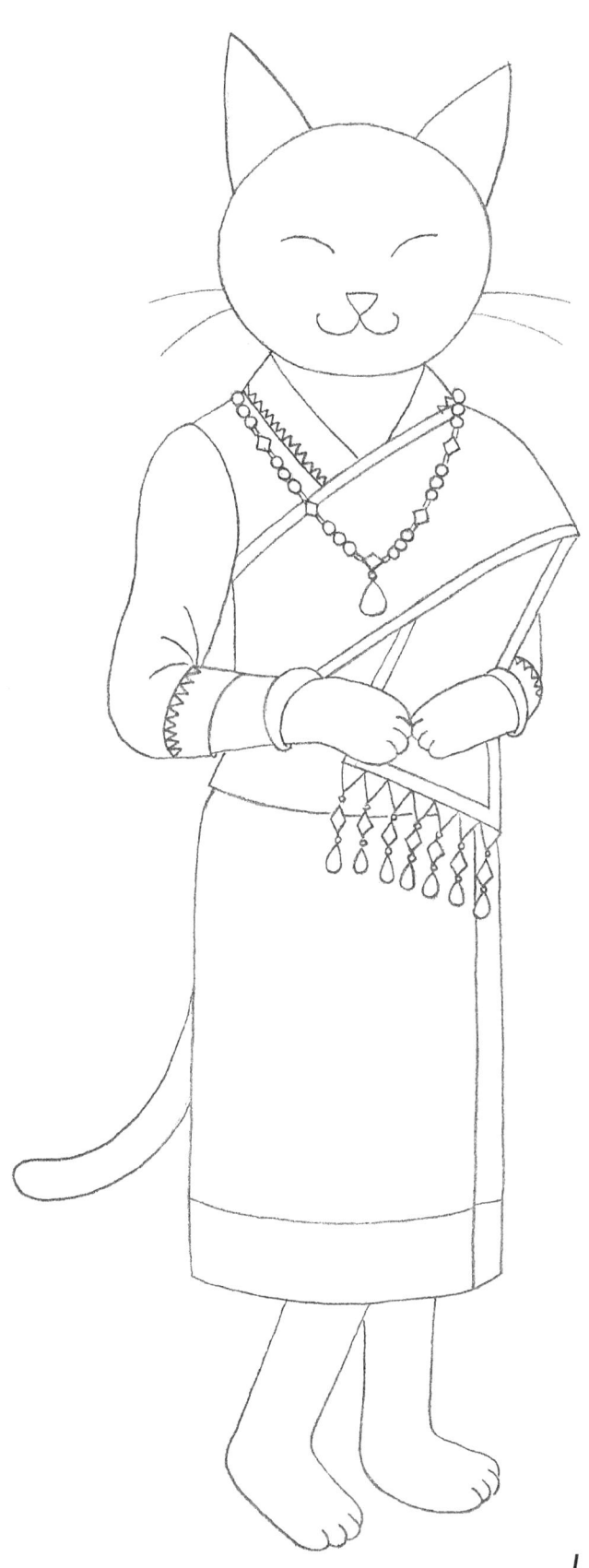

Laos Costume

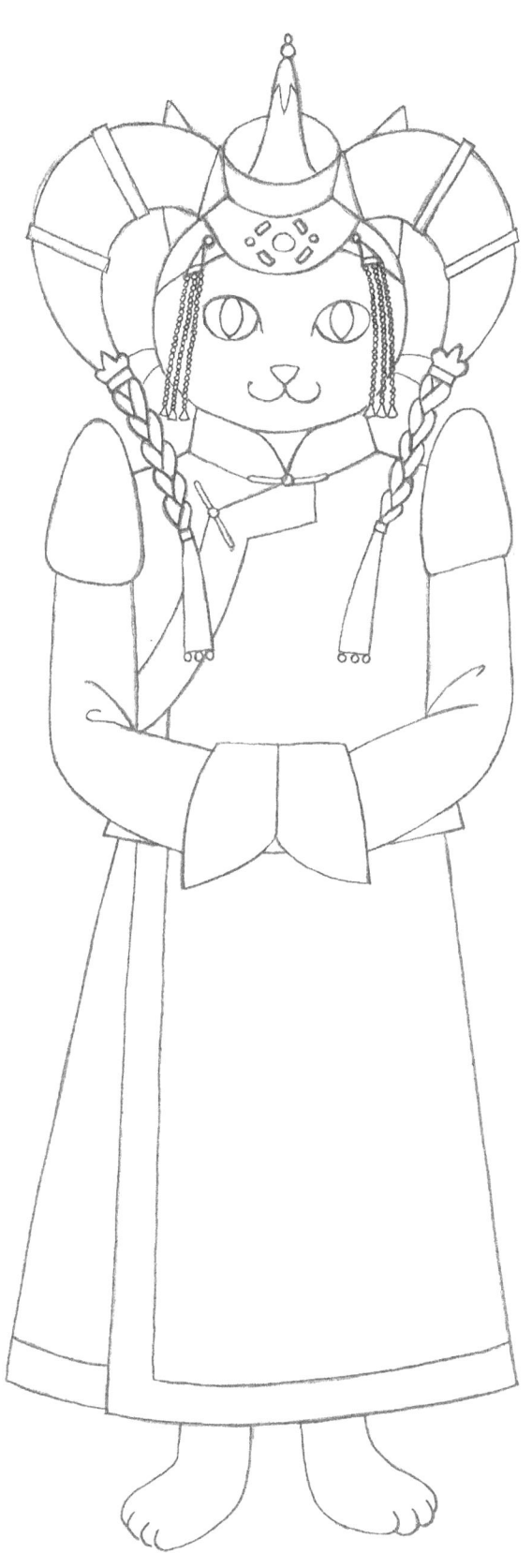

Traditional Mongolion Costume

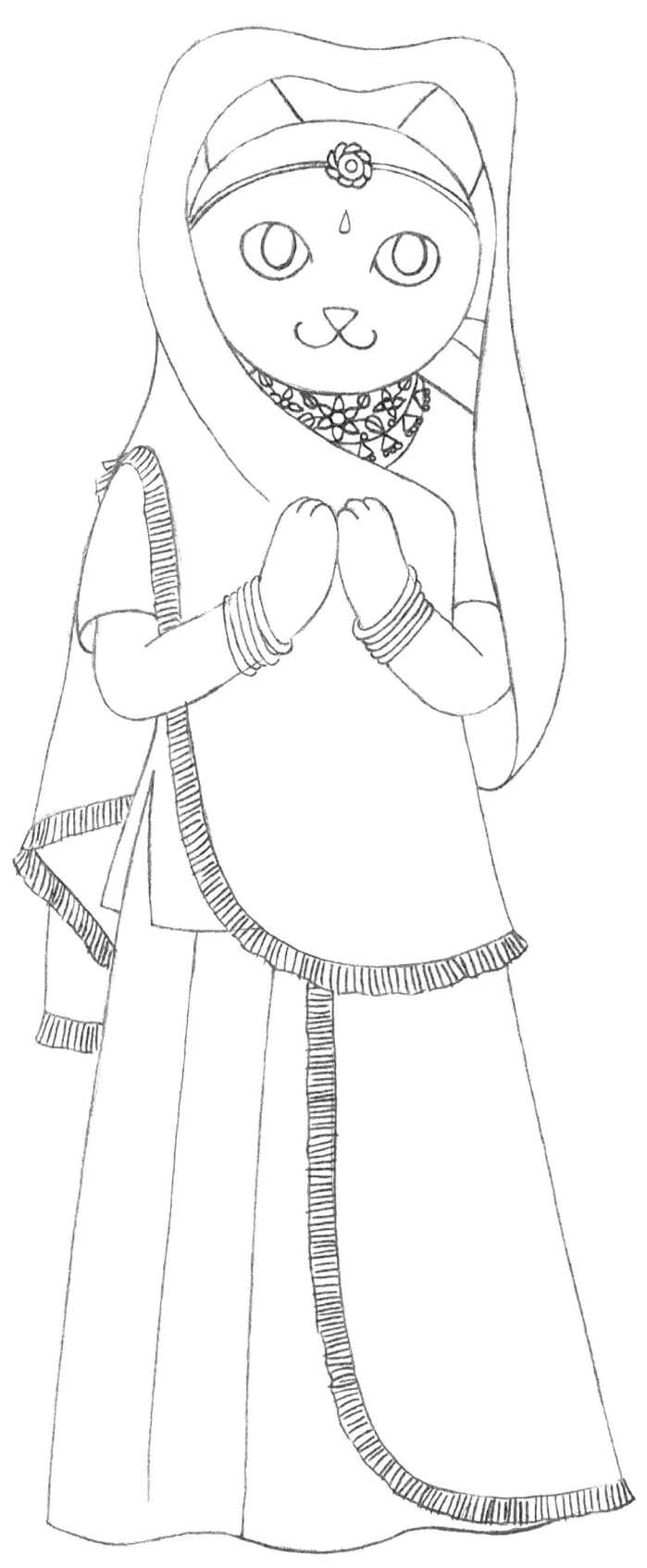

Costume of Rajasthan

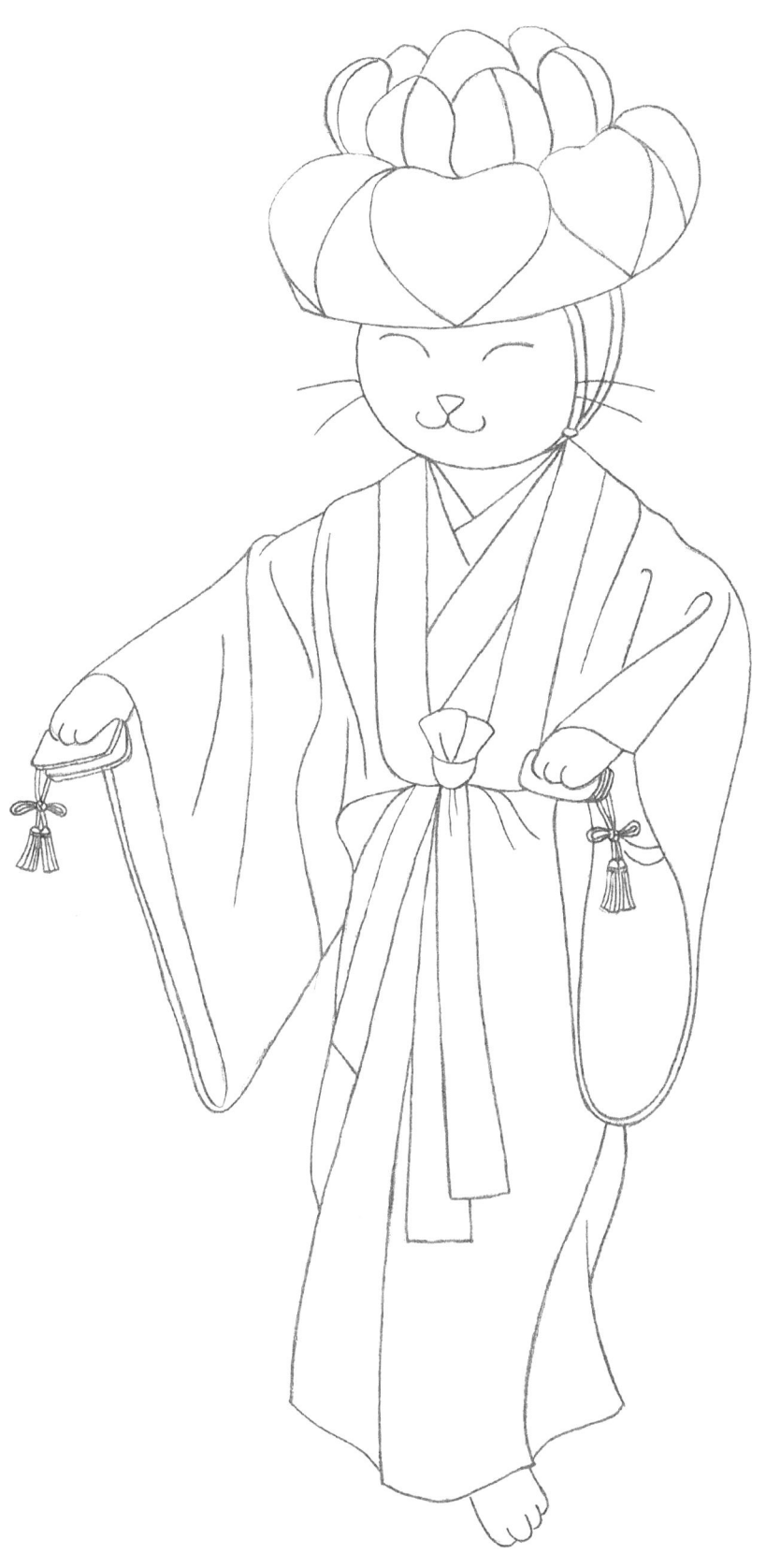

Traditional Dancing Dress of Okinawa

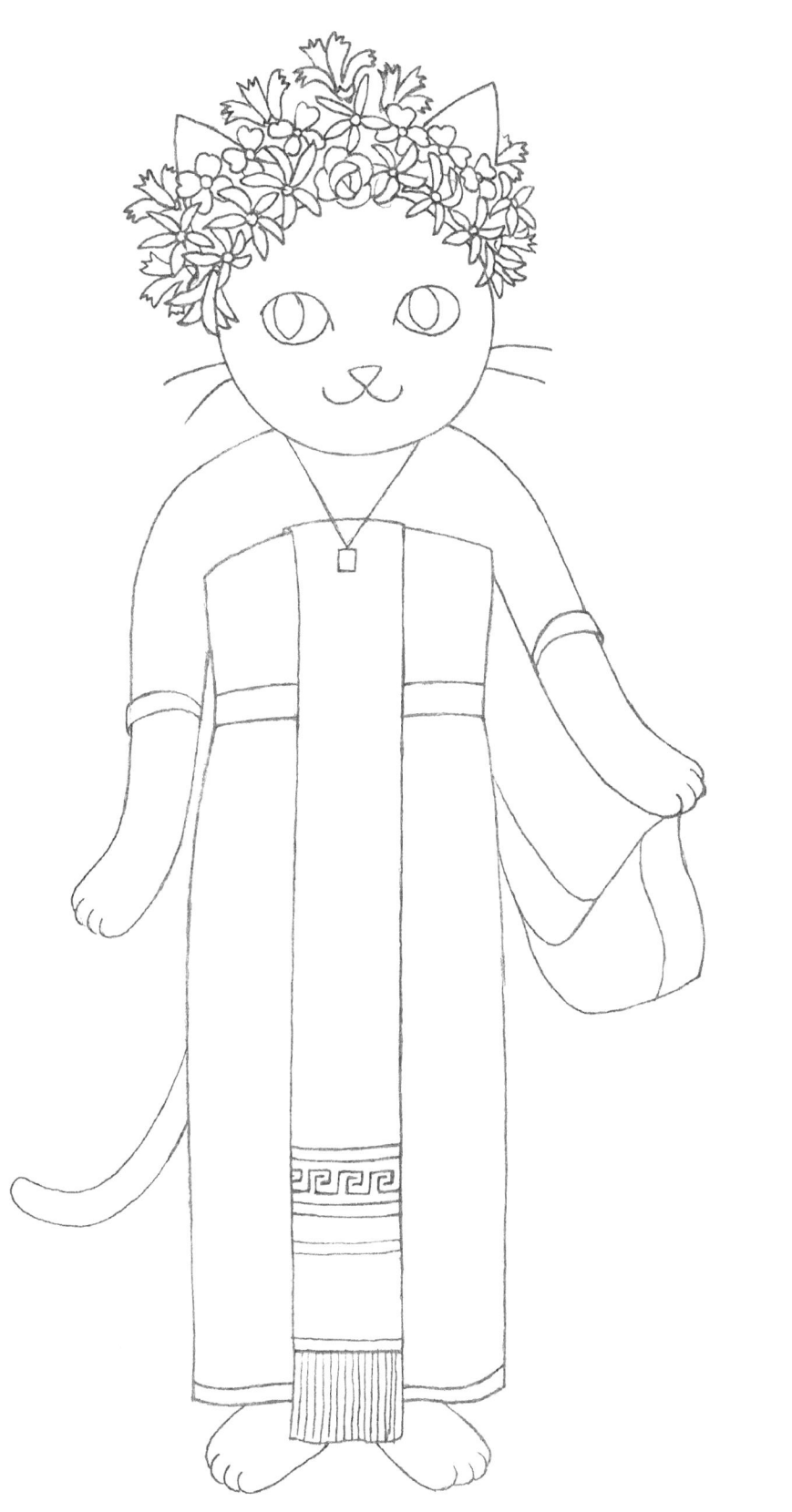

Costume of Bali

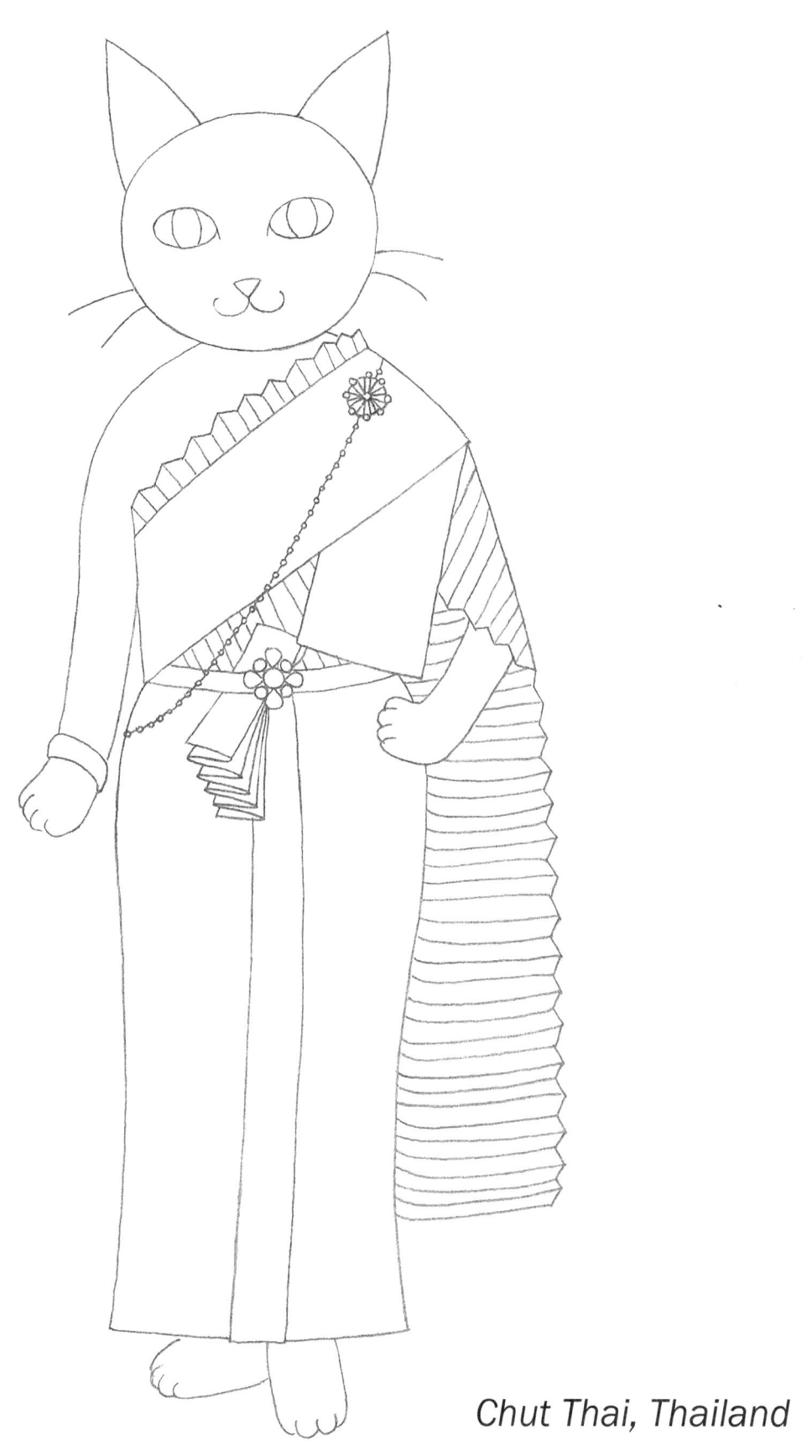

Chut Thai, Thailand

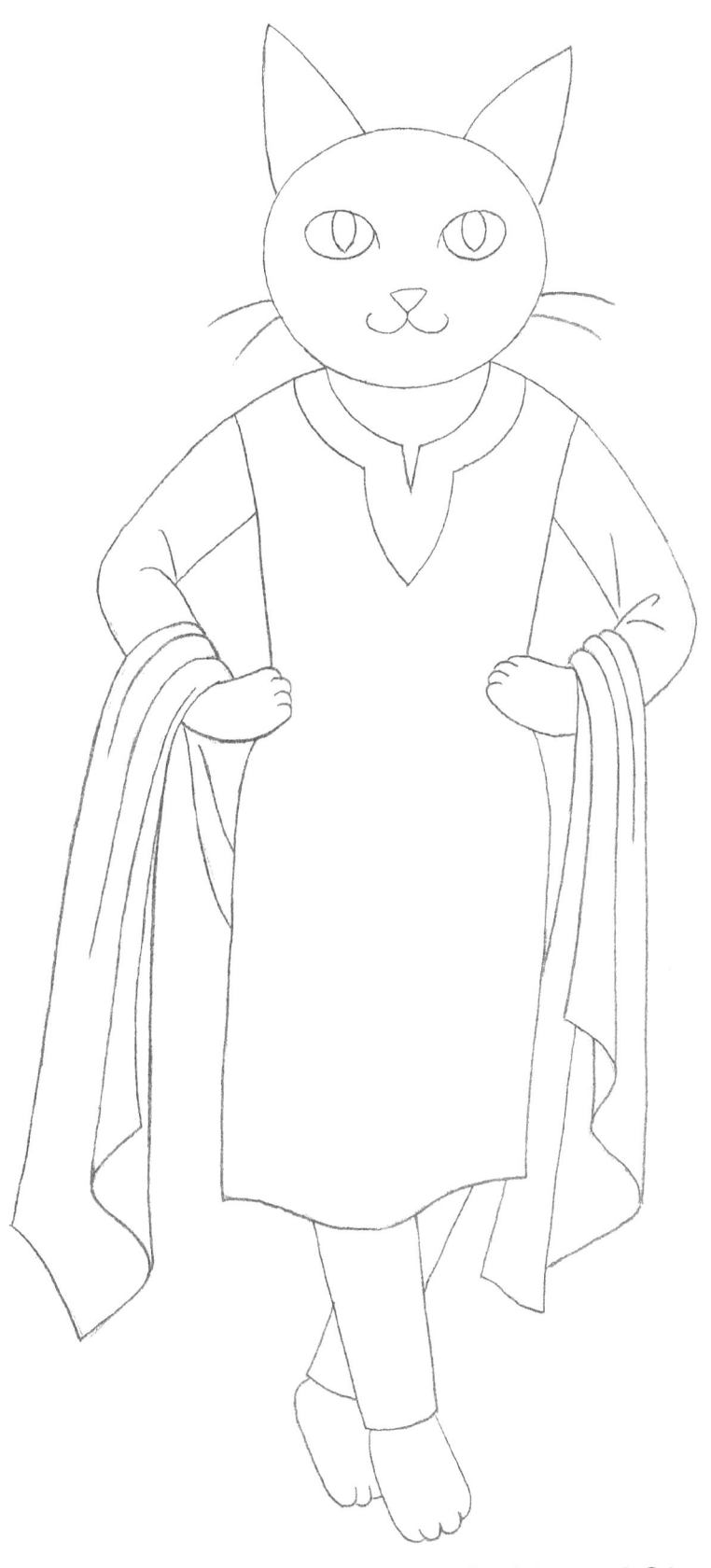

Pakistani Shalwar Kameez

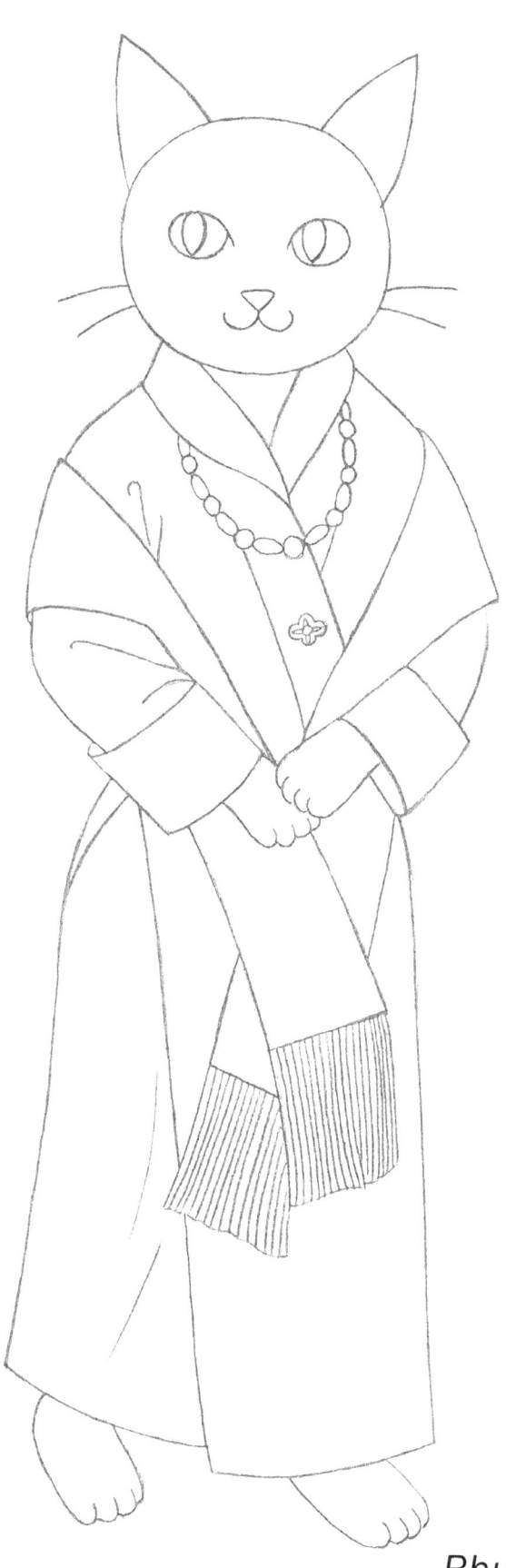

Bhutan's Costume

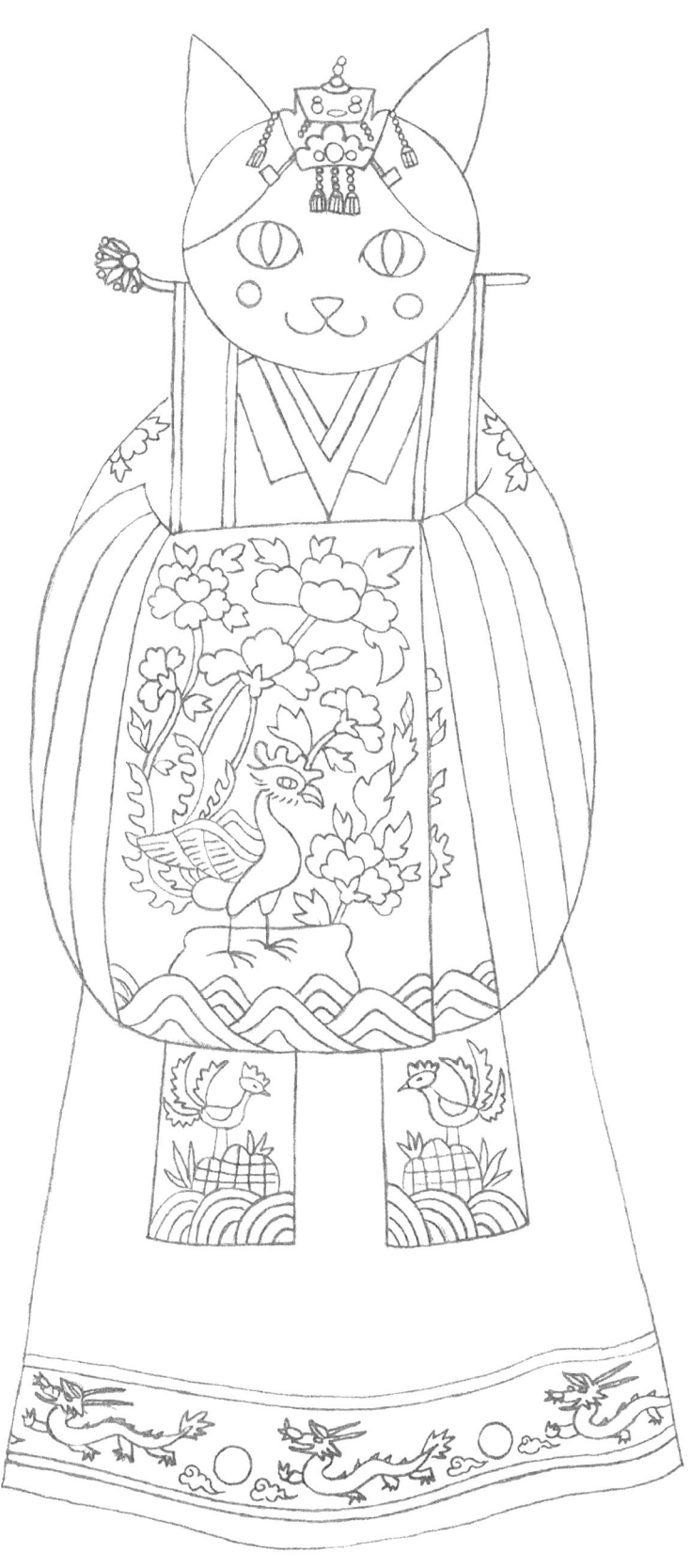

Traditional Korean Wedding Dress

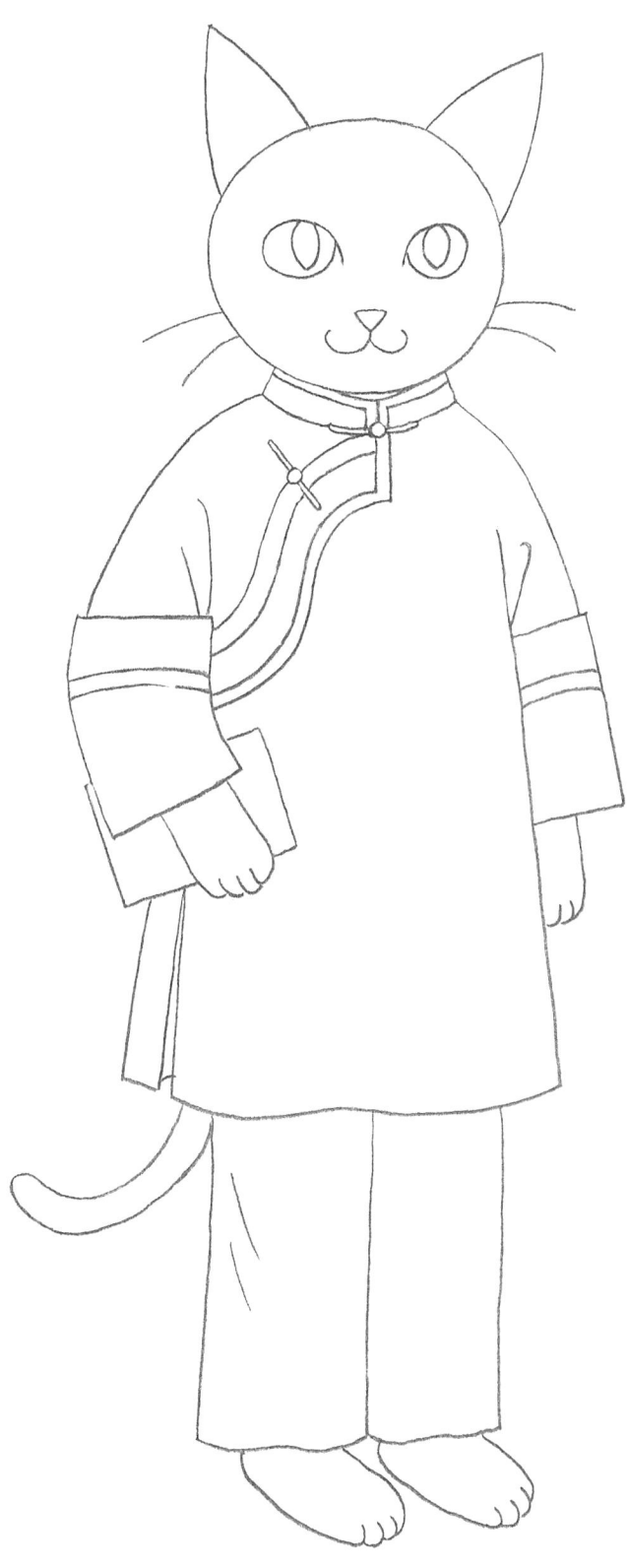

Hakka Costume, Taiwan

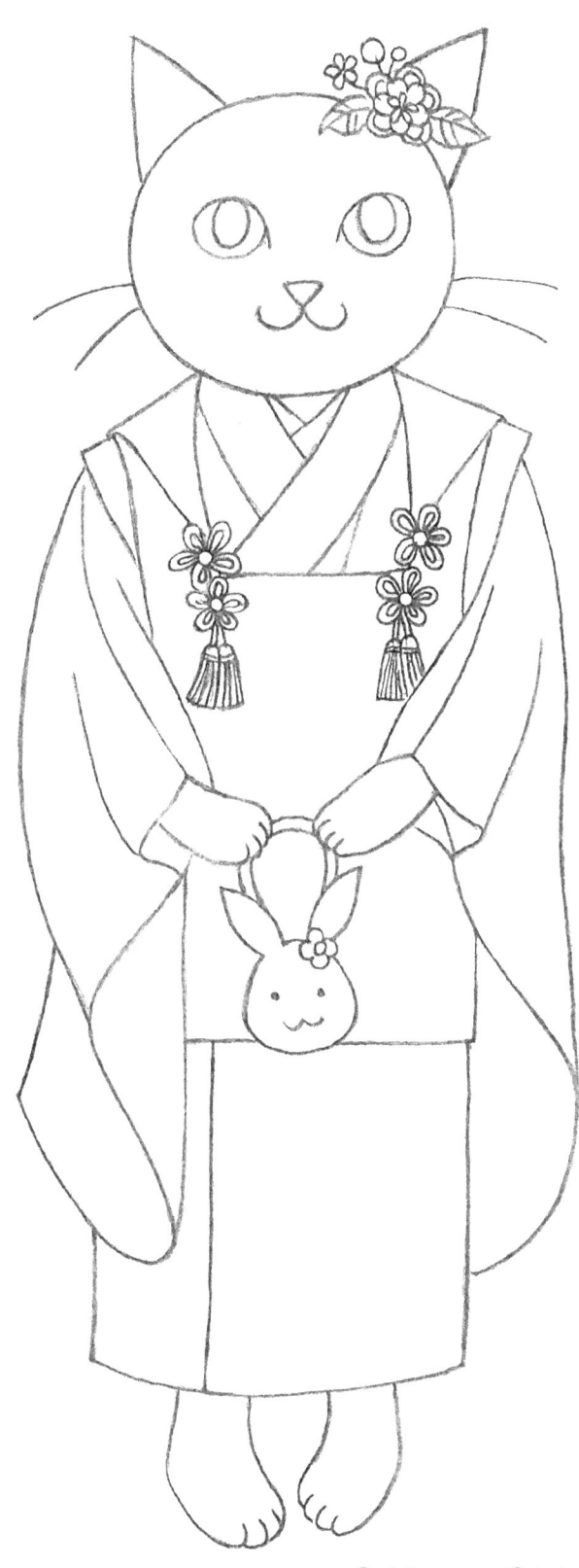

3 Years Old Girl's Kimono

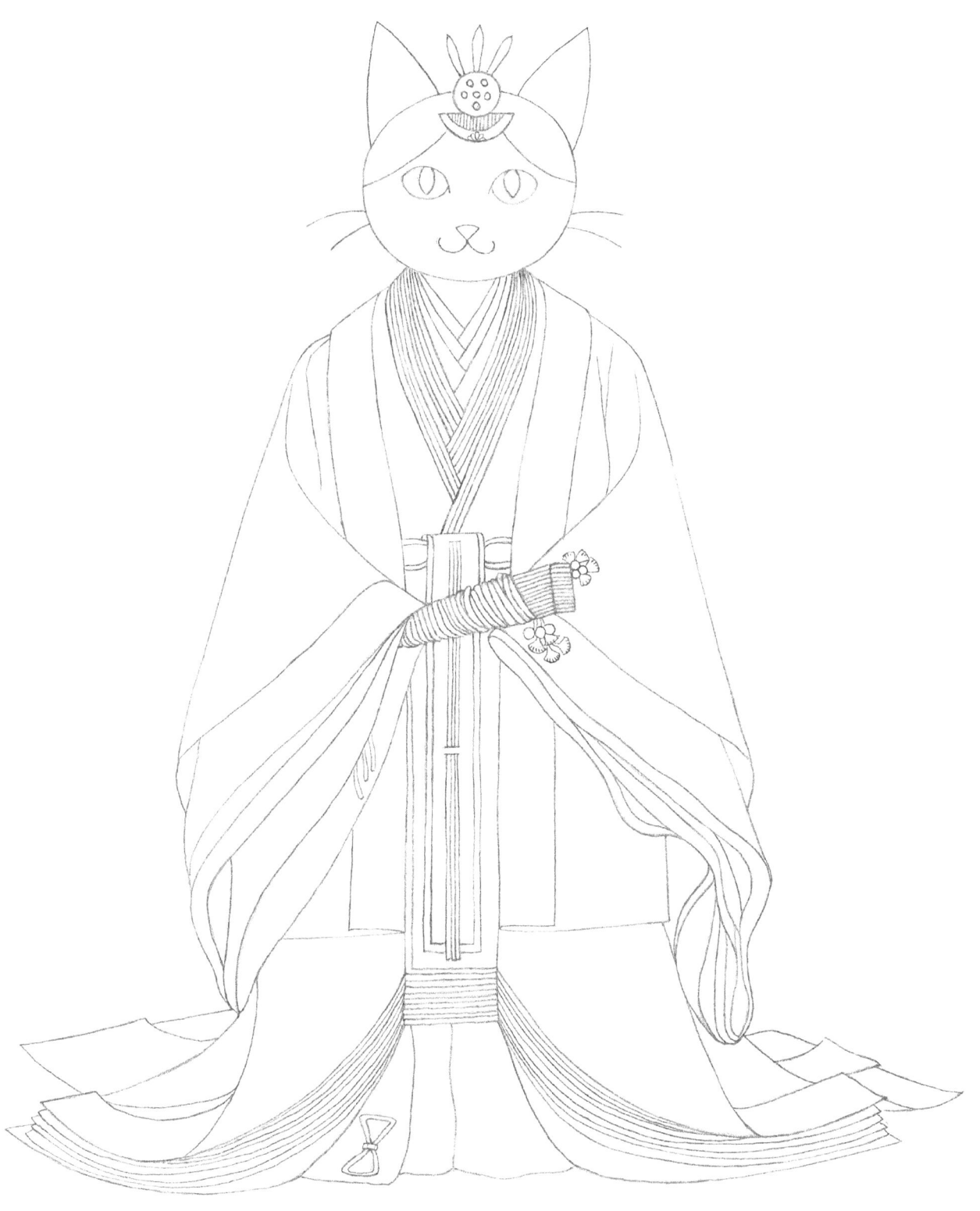

Royal Costume of Japan

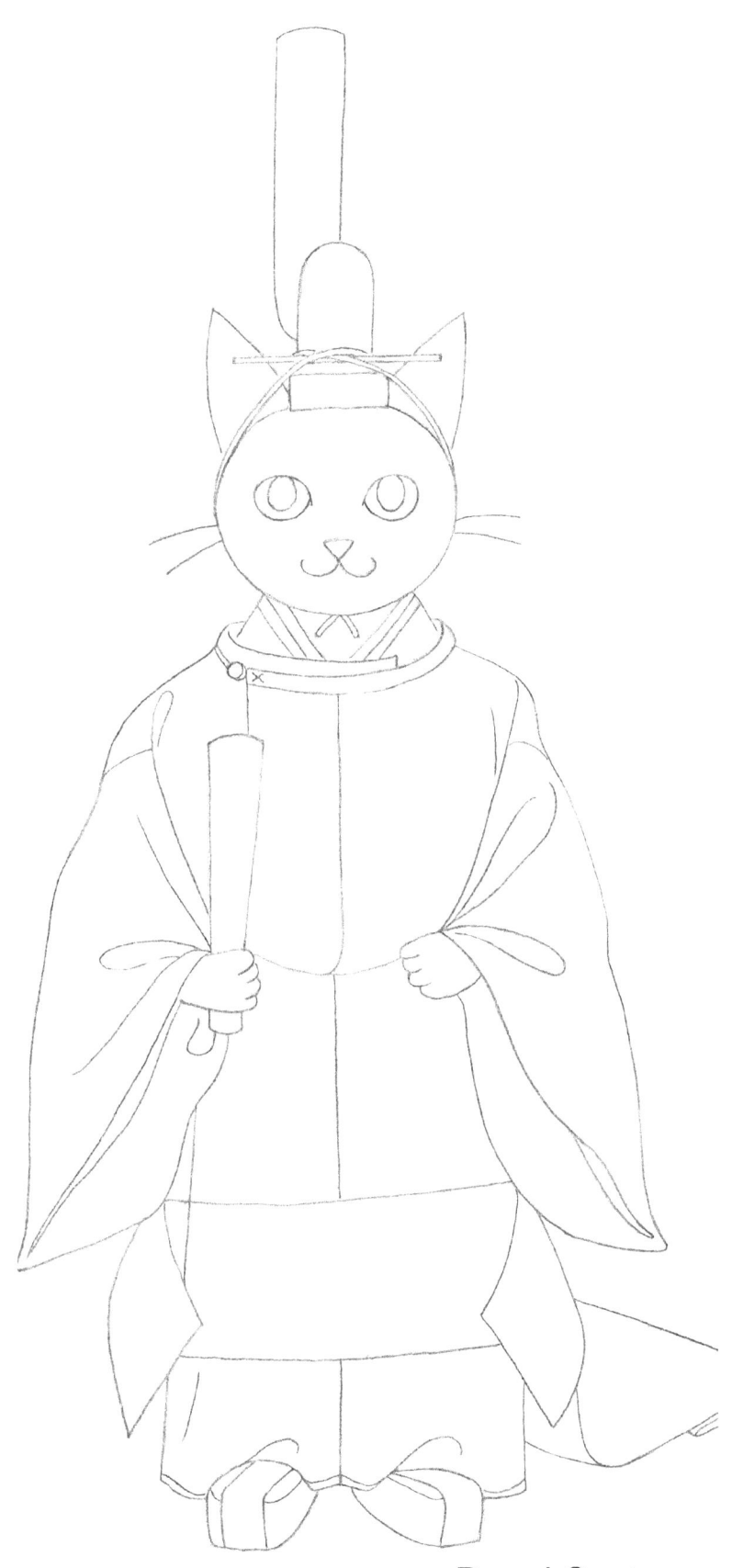

Royal Costume of Japan

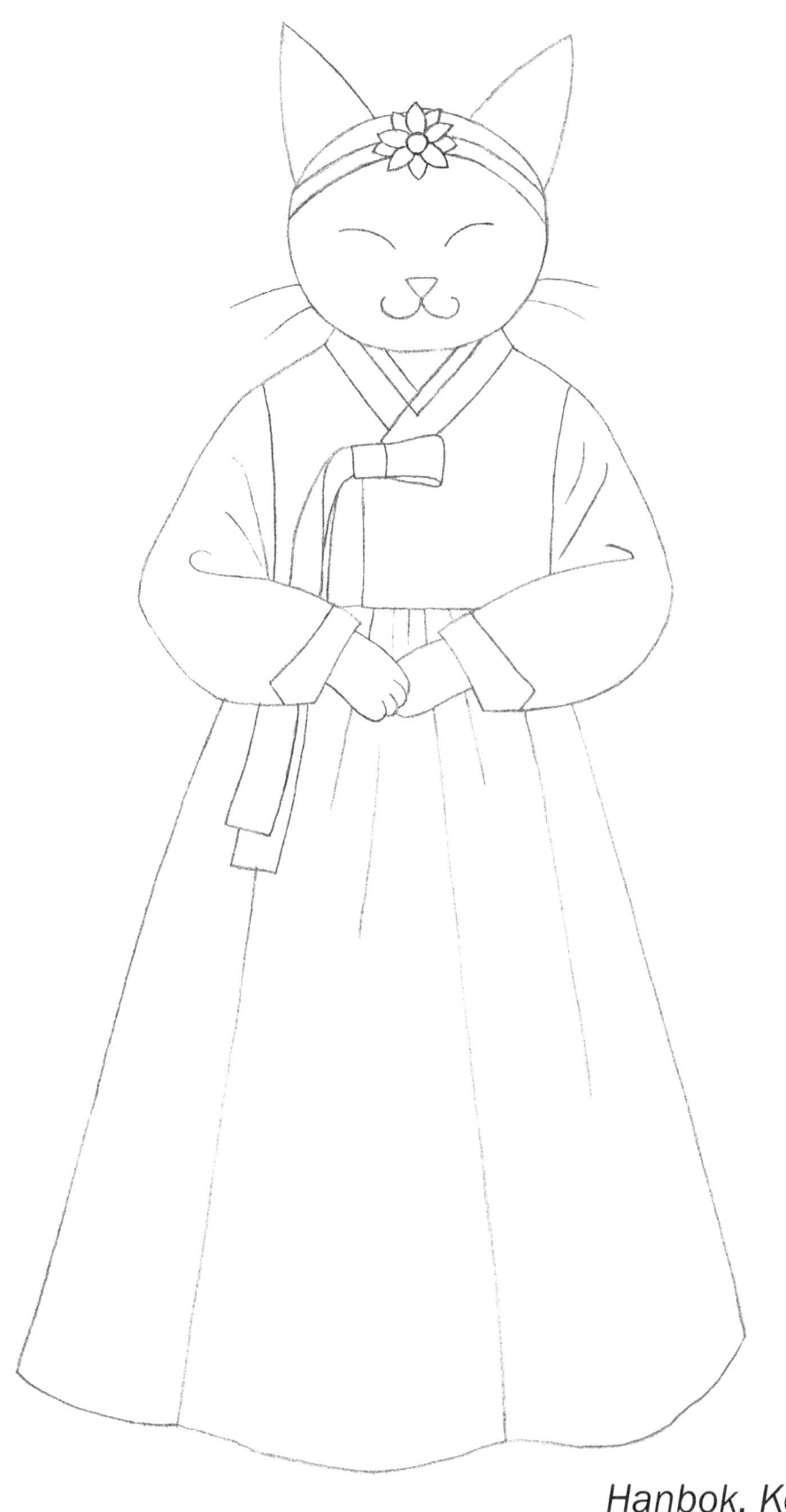

Hanbok, Korea

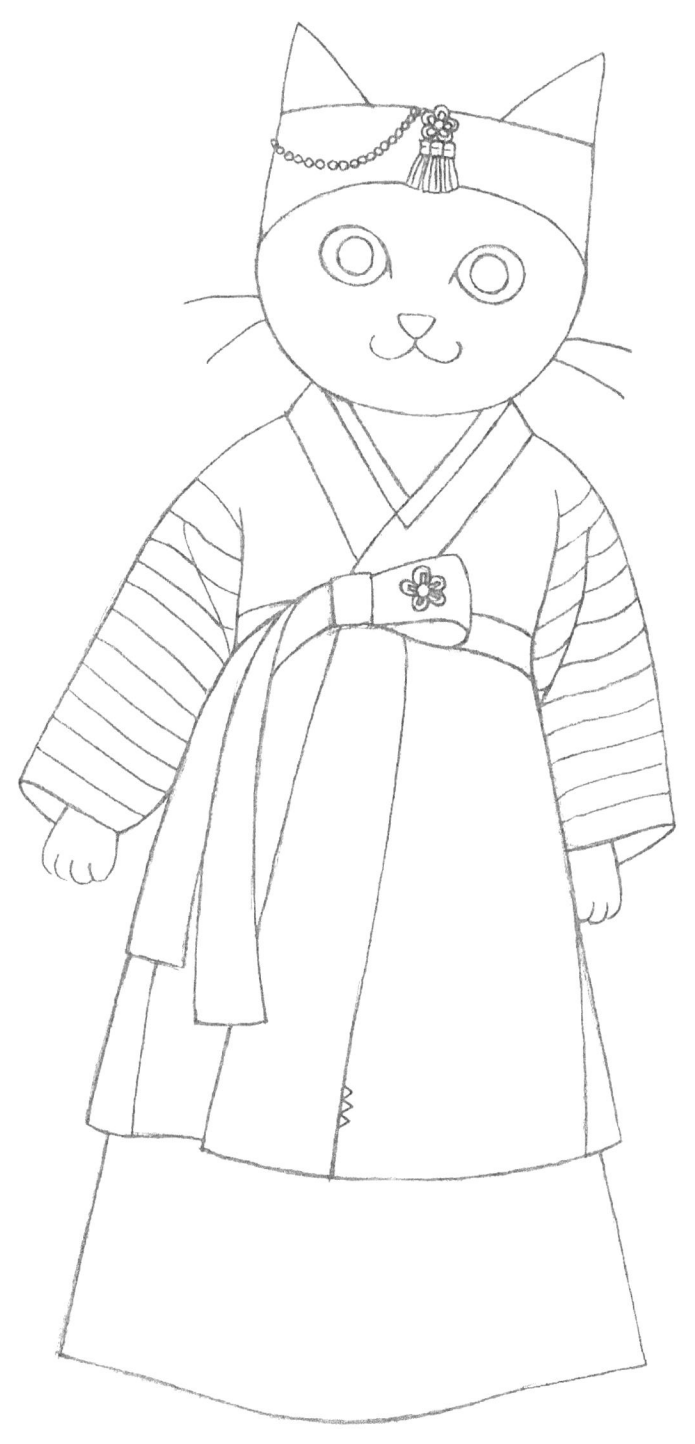

Children's Hanbok, Korea

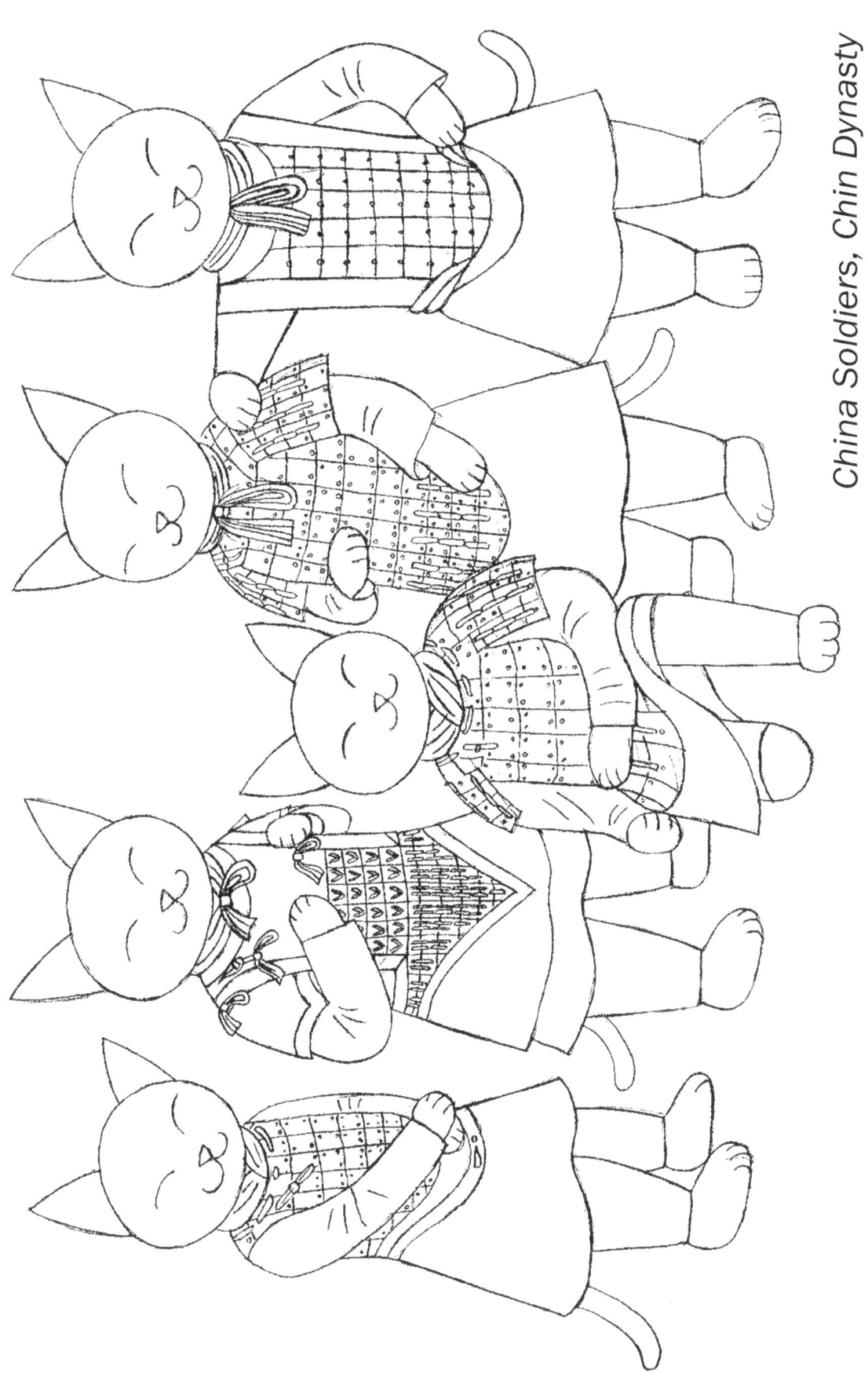

China Soldiers, Chin Dynasty

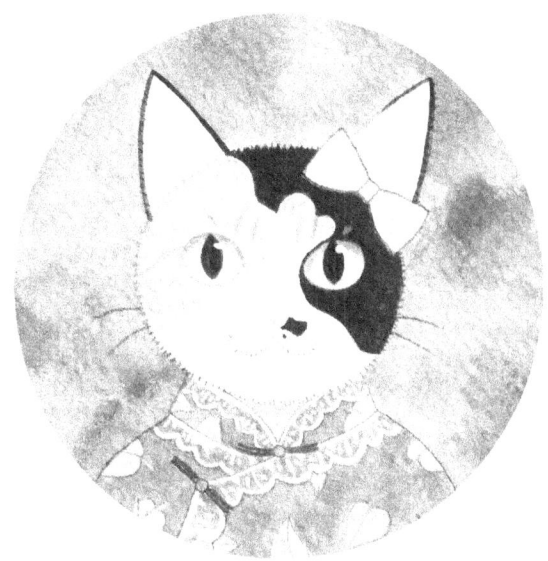

Please help to leave your review about this book so that we can improve to make our next book even better, thank you!

Visit Below Link to Get Your Digital Version

https://colokara.com/fashion01